DOLLARS
AND SENSE

A Teen Guide to
Managing Money

NICHOLAS SUIVSKI

TWENTY-FIRST CENTURY BOOKS / MINNEAPOLIS

Twenty-First Century Books™
An imprint of Lerner Publishing Group, Inc.
241 First Avenue North
Minneapolis, MN 55401 USA

For reading levels and more information, look up this title at www.lernerbooks.com.

Main body text set in Bembo Std Regular.
Typeface provided by Monotype Typography.

Library of Congress Cataloging-in-Publication Data

Names: Navarez, Vincent, author.
Title: Dollars and sense : a teen guide to managing money / Vincent Navarez.
Description: Minneapolis : Twenty-First Century Books, [2025] I Series: Fund your future I Includes bibliographical references and index. I Audience: Ages 11–18 I Audience: Grades 7–9 I Summary: "Managing money is an important skill for every teen to learn. But it can be hard to know where to start. Through engaging examples and practical strategies, discover the ins and outs of budgeting, saving, and investing"— Provided by publisher.
Identifiers: LCCN 2023038753 (print) I LCCN 2023038754 (ebook) I ISBN 9798765611326 (library binding) I ISBN 9798765630006 (paperback) I ISBN 9798765638682 (epub)
Subjects: LCSH: Finance, Personal—Juvenile literature. I Teenagers—Finance, Personal.
Classification: LCC HG179 .N376 2025 (print) I LCC HG179 (ebook) I DDC 332.02400835—dc23/eng/20230816

LC record available at https://lccn.loc.gov/2023038753
LC ebook record available at https://lccn.loc.gov/2023038754

Manufactured in the United States of America
1 – CG – 7/15/24

CONTENTS

INTRODUCTION

Managing money is important. Financial planning helps you make sure you have enough money to afford the things you need and want from food to the newest smartphone. By learning how to handle your money wisely, you can make smart choices about where to spend or save your money. As you get older, these practices can also help you grow your money to afford even bigger things, like a new car or a house. But it can be difficult to know where to start.

Just by opening this book, you've already taken a big step toward money management mastery! Throughout this book, you'll improve your financial literacy. Financial literacy means having the knowledge and skills to make good choices about money. You'll learn how to budget, save, and invest your money for your future. You'll learn practical tips and tricks for managing your money, from creating a budget to investing for the future.

By learning these skills, you can set yourself up for financial success and feel confident about managing your

Learning how to manage money now gives you a head start on some of life's biggest challenges.

money to achieve financial freedom. When you're financially free, you can live the life you want and pay for the things you need without worrying or relying on debt. *Cha-ching*!

CHAPTER ONE
Why Budget?

Have you ever wanted to buy a new bike, the latest video game, or a pair of trendy shoes, but you didn't have the money? Have your friends ever invited you on a trip, but you didn't know how to save up for it? If you're planning on going to college, you might have thought about how to start saving for college. All these things require money, and you'll need a plan to get the money to afford them.

You have probably heard of a budget. Maybe you've even tried making one in the past. It can be hard to create a budget and even harder to stick to one. But it does not have to be complicated. In this chapter, we'll explore budgeting and its importance, and how sticking to a budget can impact your life as a teen and as an adult.

What Is Budgeting?

According to Tsh Oxenreider in her book *Organized Simplicity: The Clutter-Free Approach to Intentional Living*, creating a budget is simply "telling your money where to go." Budgeting means knowing how much money you have available to you and being aware of how you spend it. It means figuring out how much money you have and how much you need for essentials (such as bills, groceries, and rent), then setting aside the rest for things you want later.

Budgeting can help you achieve your financial goals and buy the things you want without taking on unnecessary debt like big credit card bills. You've already taken a big step in the right direction just by starting this chapter. Learning to budget today can help you afford things now and set you up for financial success in the future.

Budgeting involves the whole family. Learning about spending and saving at an early age helps kids understand how to manage their own money later in life.

Why Is Budgeting Important?

Budgeting allows *you* to be in control of your money, rather than your money controlling you. Once you have built your budget, you'll have a better understanding of where your money is coming from and where it's going. This is called your financial status. A person's financial status is how much money they have (their income) and how much they spend (their expenses). It also includes a person's debt, or how much money they owe to someone else through things like loans or credit card bills.

Before you can start budgeting, you need to know your financial status. To find this, start by keeping track of your income for a month or two. Make a list or spreadsheet of every dollar you get, from money you make at a job to cash your grandma sent in your birthday card. Then make another list of your expenses, the things you pay for, including regular ones like phone bills or transportation costs. Also include occasional expenses, such as movie tickets or eating out. As these lists grow, you will get a clearer picture of where your money is coming from and where it is going.

Next, make a list of your financial assets and liabilities. An asset is something you own that has value. Liability is a responsibility you have or a debt that you owe. Make a list of what you own, such as savings or valuable possessions, as well as any debts you owe. Did you borrow money from your sister to buy a new shirt? Write it down! Understanding your assets and liabilities will help you measure your overall financial status.

It is also important to know where your money is going once you have it. You can do this by tracking your spending habits. Then you can evaluate your financial situation, decide if you can cut out unnecessary spending, and save more money.

Once you know where your money is, it's time to set some goals.

Short-term vs. Long-term Goals

Setting goals is an essential part of budgeting. Goals give you a clear direction and purpose for managing your money. They act as a guide to help you stay focused, motivated, and disciplined in your budgeting efforts.

There are two types of goals: short-term and long-term. Short-term goals identify what you want to achieve in the near future, such as this weekend or next month. You might want to save money to replace an old pair of headphones or just go out to dinner with your friends. These goals may appear small, but setting these short-term goals will help you develop healthy habits and build progress toward bigger goals.

Long-term goals may take months or even years to complete. It takes a long time to save up enough money to buy a car or go to college. These goals demand more planning and commitment over a long period of time. Long-term goals can also help you know how much money you can spend now and still achieve your future goals.

Be S.M.A.R.T. and Stay Focused

A goal can be as simple as buying a new phone. But some goals are more helpful than others. Setting S.M.A.R.T. goals can help you make sure your goals are not only possible with

Setting aside even a few dollars a month can help you reach your long-term financial goals.

your budget, but also help you create an effective plan to achieve them. S.M.A.R.T. is short for Specific, Measurable, Achievable, Relevant, and Time Bound. When setting goals, make sure to check that they are:

- *Specific:* Financial goals should be clear and well-defined. For example, you could save $10 monthly to buy a new video game ($60) in six months.
- *Measurable:* Financial goals should be countable. This helps you track your progress and know

when you have achieved it. Seeing your progress may encourage you to keep saving, which is helpful when you are tempted to spend more than your budget allows. Create a spreadsheet or a checklist to help you stay on track.

- *Achievable:* Financial goals should be realistic. If a goal doesn't fit your budget, it can be very disappointing when you don't achieve it. But making financial plans can also show you that something you thought was too expensive could actually be within your budget. Make a simple and realistic saving plan you can follow. For example, if you are earning $100 a week, setting a goal to save $1,000 every month is unrealistic.
- *Relevant:* Financial goals should align with your overall financial goals and priorities. Suppose your goal is to save up for a trip with your friends. But saving for this trip might mean not saving for other things, such as your college fund or building up emergency funds. Knowing your priorities will help you make these tough decisions.
- *Time-bound:* Financial goals must have a deadline and a specific target to be successful. If you don't know how long you'll be saving money for, you may be more likely to break your budget for more short-term spending. For example, if you want to buy a $300 mountain bike, you could plan to save $50 every month for six months to save up for it. Now you know exactly when you'll be getting that new bike!

Create a Plan

What happens if your S.M.A.R.T. goals don't fit your budget? Do you have to give them up? Not necessarily. In addition to saving the money you already have, you can also find ways to earn extra money, such as doing yard work for neighbors or selling clothes you've outgrown. Increasing your income can help you reach your goal faster! Knowing your budget and setting S.M.A.R.T. goals will help you determine if this extra income will help you save enough money.

You can also consider opening a separate savings account at your local bank for this goal. Depositing the money into a separate savings account can keep it safe and prevent you from accidentally spending it.

Avoid Debt and Overspending

Have you ever borrowed money from a friend when you forgot your wallet at home? This is an example of debt. Debt is the money you owe to someone else. Even if you've never been in debt, it's important to understand what debt is and how it can impact your financial future.

Paying back a debt to a friend is usually pretty simple. But when you borrow money from an institution such as a bank or a credit card company, you usually have to pay an extra fee called interest. Interest is like a rental fee for the money you borrowed, and it is usually a percentage of the amount you borrowed. It's important to know what that interest rate is so that you don't lose track of how much you owe the bank or credit card company. Not paying off the interest can cause your debt to get bigger and bigger over time.

If you need a loan, make sure you understand the interest rates and how they will affect your ability to repay the amount over time. Budgeting can help you avoid unnecessary debt. Avoiding high-interest debt can also help you be more financially stable and avoid getting into more debt than you can afford.

Types of Debt

There are many types of debt you can take on from financial institutions. High-interest debt means you have to pay back a lot of extra money for the money you borrowed, which makes it hard to pay off what you owe. For example, if you borrow $50 from your sister and promise to pay her back with 50 percent interest, you'll end up paying her a total of $75. That's a lot more money! You're basically paying $25 extra to purchase something worth $50. Think of what you could have done instead with that extra $25!

Credit card debt is one type of high-interest debt. If you borrow money on a credit card and don't pay it back before the first billing date, you must pay back a lot of extra money on top of what you borrowed. Some credit cards charge up to 25 percent interest.

Payday loans are even worse. Some payday loans charge up to 400 percent interest!

Low-interest debt has interest rates usually around 8 percent or below. Low-interest debts are usually easier to manage and can help you pay for big things over a long period of time.

Mortgages are a type of low-interest loan that many people use to buy a home. The interest rates on mortgages are usually lower than on credit cards. Other types of low-interest debt can include some car loans and federal student loans.

Plan and Prepare for the Future

There are many things you might want to achieve as you get older. Maybe you'll want to buy a car, move into your first apartment or house, save for college or trade school, take a solo trip, or make a big purchase. Budgeting helps you plan for things you want while also preparing for unforeseen events.

Think of a time your family planned a vacation. You may have started by deciding where to go, booked your transport and accommodations, and then planned your activities. This is similar to financial planning. Financial planning simply means setting money goals and making plans to reach them. You must research your goals, create a timeline for reaching them, and decide how much money you need to achieve them.

The best travel planners also prepare for the unexpected. They build an emergency fund into their budgets to deal with surprises like losing luggage or canceled flights. Good financial planners do the same thing. It's a good idea to have at least $500, or three to six months of regular expenses, saved in an emergency fund. Having money saved for emergencies can help you avoid using a credit card and getting into high-interest debt.

Tips for Making Budgeting Work for You

1. *Start Small.* Track one category of spending, such as food or entertainment, for a month or two. Did you spend more or less than you expected? Once you have the hang of it, add another category to track.
2. *Get Creative.* Find fun and rewarding ways to save money. Make your own coffee at home instead of buying it at a coffee shop. Host a potluck dinner with friends instead of going to a restaurant.
3. *Involve Your Friends.* Encourage your friends to join you in budgeting. Sticking to your budget is easier if your friends are on board too.
4. *Prioritize Your Goals.* Do you need to save for a new phone or a fun day at an amusement park? Decide what's essential and prioritize spending accordingly.
5. *Be Realistic.* Set a goal to save money according to your expenses. You can't save much money when you have a lot of expenses every month. Adjust your goals as needed.
6. *Stay Positive.* Budgeting is challenging, but it's also rewarding. Celebrate your successes, whether big or small. The more you consistently budget, the easier it will get!

CHAPTER TWO

Budgeting Pros and Cons

W hen school, friends, family, and extracurricular activities take up a lot of your time, budgeting and saving might seem like just another chore. But learning to manage your money can actually save you time.

Imagine you're preparing for a big test. Would you go into the exam without studying? Or would you prepare by reviewing the material? Getting a good grade requires time management and preparation. Budgeting works the same way. Taking the time to create a budget and sticking to your financial plan will help you get an A+ in successful money management.

The Benefits of Budgeting

Taking control of your finances doesn't just help you afford fun things. It is also empowering, builds confidence, and helps your mental health. With budgeting, you can always know exactly how much money you make each month and where it goes. This can help avoid stress and allow you to spend confidently. By effectively managing your budget, you can also create a sense of trust and

Setting financial goals and making good decisions on how to spend and save your money helps you maintain a stress-free life.

responsibility with people who could lend you money.

Having a plan helps you worry less about unexpected expenses. When you set aside a specific amount each month, you make progress toward your financial goals without feeling anxious or overwhelmed about how to pay for them. And with fewer worries about money, you can devote more time to other aspects of your life.

The Difficulties of Not Budgeting

Not having a budget is like going on a road trip without directions. You'll probably get lost or end up miles from your destination. Just as getting lost can lead to wasted time and frustration, not having a budget can lead to overspending and debt that pushes your goals further into the future. Overspending is when you spend more money than you budgeted for. Morgan Housel states in *The Psychology of Money* that "spending money to show people how much money you

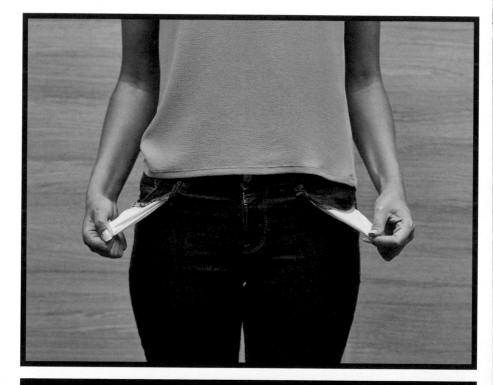

Finding yourself with no money to buy things you want or pay for fun activities is frustrating. Budgeting and careful planning can help you avoid this frustration.

have is the fastest way to have less money." This can lead to debt and financial problems.

Financial troubles due to not budgeting may also impact your relationships. Consider a few examples:

- *Friends:* Overspending on social outings can strain your friendships. You may feel pressure to spend money on expensive activities or gifts to fit in with your friends, even if it's beyond your budget. This can lead to financial stress and even bad feelings toward your friends. Instead, communicate with your friends about your financial situation and find affordable activities you can enjoy together.
- *Family:* Not budgeting can also hurt family relationships. It can be hard to keep asking your parents or guardians for money, and they may get upset if they think you're being irresponsible. Creating and sticking to a budget shows maturity and responsibility. This may make your parents or guardians more comfortable giving you spending money.
- *Future Relationships:* Not budgeting can even impact your future relationships. Money is one of the most common things couples disagree about. Spending too much will often lead to disagreements and trust issues. By practicing healthy money habits now, you can be prepared to build a strong, healthy relationship with your future partner.

Different Methods of Budgeting— Which Suits You Best?

- *Traditional Budgeting:* This is the most common type of personal budgeting. In traditional budgeting, you set aside a specific amount of money for different expenses, such as entertainment, groceries, rent or mortgage payments, transportation, utilities, and things that don't fit into any of the other categories. You track your spending and adjust your budget as needed.

Traditional budgeting is simple and straightforward. It gives you a clear picture of how much you have and how much you need to spend each month.

- *50/30/20 Budgeting:* In this method, you split
  your income into three groups. Fifty percent of
  your money goes in the first group, often for
  basic needs such as groceries, rent/mortgage,
  and utilities. The second category, 30 percent, is
  used for things you want, but don't necessarily
  need, such as dining out, entertainment, and
  gym memberships. The last 20 percent is put
  into savings. This money can be saved for the
  future, repay debts, and have a backup in case
  of emergencies.
- *The Envelope Method:* This type of budgeting
  involves dividing cash into different envelopes
  based on different categories of expenses.
  These categories might be things such as food,
  transportation, entertainment, clothing, and
  savings. You should choose categories that
  make sense with your current situation. With
  this method, you only use the money in each
  envelope for that specific category of expenses.
  This can help you visualize how much you are
  spending and saving, but it does require taking
  out cash to use for these expenses.
- *Zero-Sum Budgeting:* A zero-sum budget
  tracks all income in a specific time period,
  such as one month, and puts everything into
  different categories of expenses and savings.
  This method is called "zero-sum" because it
  involves allocating every dollar of your income,
  ensuring that your income minus your expenses
  equals zero.

These are only a few examples of the many types of budgets. It's important to figure out the right type of budget that meets your needs. When deciding on a budgeting method, consider your financial goals. For example, if you need to repay debt right away, use a zero-sum budgeting method to allocate as much of your income as possible to debt repayment. But if you want to save for something long-term, like a down payment on a house, try 50/30/20 budgeting and allocate 20 percent of every paycheck to savings.

How you spend money can help you choose the best budgeting method for you. If you tend to overspend in one category, such as clothes or entertainment, consider an envelope budgeting method that limits your spending in that category. If your spending is different every month, consider a zero-sum budgeting method that lets you track every dollar and make changes as needed.

Your chosen budgeting method should also be one that matches your lifestyle. This will make it easier to follow. For example, if you prefer using cash, the envelope budgeting method might be the best for you.

The Pros and Cons of Budgeting Methods

There are pros and cons to every budgeting method. To see if a budgeting method fits your financial lifestyle, use this table to understand its advantages and disadvantages.

Table 1. The Pros and Cons of Budgeting Methods		
Method	**Pros**	**Cons**
Traditional Budgeting	• simple and easy to implement • allocates money to different expenses, tracks spending, and adjusts the budget as needed	• time-consuming to track expenses and adjust the budget
50/30/20 Budgeting	• simple and easy to follow • encourages saving and can help prevent overspending on unnecessary expenses	• not suitable for those with living expenses that are more than 50 percent, or those who need to save more than 20 percent • too rigid for some people who prefer more flexibility in their budget
Envelope Method	• requires careful planning and goal setting • prevents overspending on specific categories of expenses • provides a tangible way to visualize and manage your spending	• not practical for those who prefer to use digital payment methods • time-consuming to separate cash into different envelopes
Zero-Sum Budgeting	• ensures that every dollar is allocated and helps prevent overspending • prioritizes debt repayment or savings goals	• challenging and more strict, leaves no room for unassigned money • does not account for unexpected expenses or changes in income

Common Budgeting Challenges

Creating and sticking to a budget can be challenging. Sometimes things happen that we didn't expect. But there are strategies you can use to be prepared for almost anything that comes your way. These are some common challenges in budgeting and some strategies to help you overcome them.

Unexpected Expenses

Unexpected expenses are, well, unexpected! Even the most prepared budgeters can be blindsided by emergency expenses. However, building a fund to cover unexpected costs can keep you from disrupting your entire budget. Aim to save at least three to six months' worth of expenses in your emergency fund as a safety net.

Lifestyle Changes

Lifestyle changes, such as starting college or getting a new job, can also affect your budget. These can be exciting! However, it is important to adjust your budget to reflect your new needs. For example, you might need to spend more on transportation to get to a new job, or you may need to save up for college textbooks. You may need to reevaluate your expenses or increase your income by getting a job on the weekends or over the summer.

Overspending

Overspending can present a big challenge. Discipline and careful planning can help you avoid overspending. This may include tracking your expenses, identifying categories where you tend to overspend, and looking for ways to cut back on

Car trouble doesn't have to slow you down. Having some money set aside for unexpected repairs will keep you moving forward.

expenses. For example, you can create a more strict spending plan to reduce food costs or cancel unnecessary subscriptions. You can also find an accountability partner—a friend, study partner, parent, or guardian—to help you keep on track. You might find yourself making progress more easily when you have someone to celebrate with.

Lack of Financial Literacy

It's important to have the skills to understand your money. There are lots of online resources, classes, and books that you can use to learn about budgeting. These resources can help you develop better financial and budgeting knowledge.

CHAPTER THREE
Building and Using a Budget

Building a budget can be a fun and rewarding process, much like building a model airplane or finishing a puzzle. Just like these activities, budgeting requires careful planning, problem-solving, and focus.

This chapter teaches you how to approach budgeting as a creative challenge. You will discover how budgeting can help you achieve your dreams and reach your goals with practical tips and real-life examples. You'll learn how to make the most of your money and help turn your financial goals into reality.

Budgeting: Start Now, Prosper Later

Step 1: Track Your Income and Expenses

Choose a period of time, such as one month or one week. Monitor how much money you have coming in and going out during that time. Write down the income you received, such as an allowance, part-time jobs, babysitting money, and birthday gifts. Then write down your expenses during that

BUDGET FOR WEEK(S) OF **6/14–6/21**

INCOME		
Income Source	**Planned Amount**	**Actual Earned**
Allowance	$15	$15
Paycheck	$100	$100
Birthday $$	$20	$25
Totals:	$135	$140

EXPENSES			
Expense	**Planned Amount**	**Actual Spent**	**Leak or Leftover**
Snacks	$10	$13.89	-$3.89
Cell bill	$45	$55.69	-$10.69
B-day gift	$25	$22.50	+$2.50
Pay back Jen	$15	$15	$0
Totals:	$95	$107.08	-$12.08

SAVINGS	
Planned Savings:	$20
Leftover Money Not Spent:	$12.92
Actual Money Put Into Savings:	$20
Money to Carry Over to Next Budget Cycle:	$12.92

A weekly budget is a picture of how much money you have, how much you are spending, and what areas might need to be adjusted.

time, such as lunch money, phone bills, sports equipment, or gifts for friends. Add up how much you had coming in and going out.

Step 2: Identify Fixed and Variable Expenses

Now that you've written down your expenses, you can separate them into fixed and variable expenses. Fixed expenses occur regularly and usually do not change from month to month. These expenses might be things such as monthly car payments, regular school or activity fees, music streaming subscriptions, and gym membership fees.

In contrast, variable expenses change from month to month. These expenses may include coffee or lunch outings, entertainment expenses such as movies, concerts, and books, and utility expenses that change, such as a cell phone plan that charges based on how much data you use.

Go back to the list you made in Step 1. See if you can categorize your expenses as "fixed" or "variable." Were you surprised by the results?

Step 3: Decide How Much Money to Budget for Each Category

Now that you know how much money you receive and spend every month, you can make a budget for each category. Start by prioritizing your fixed expenses, bills, and anything else that is the most important to you. Decide which fixed expenses are necessary and how much you would like to spend on each of those categories. Use the remaining income to allocate funds for variable expenses. Be careful not to budget more than your income!

Step 4: Incorporate Your Savings Goals

Remember to make a category for savings. How much do you want to save every month? We'll talk about this more in the next chapter, so it's okay to just make an estimate for now.

Sticking to Your Budget: Tips and Strategies

Tips for Staying Motivatod

It can be challenging to stay motivated when trying to cut back on expenses. However, it's essential to keep your goals in mind. When you feel unmotivated, try creating a vision board or chart to visualize and remind yourself of the bigger picture.

Strategies for Staying on Track

One strategy for sticking to a budget is using cash instead of digital wallets or credit cards. When you actually see the money leaving your hand, it will encourage you to stay within your budget. Budgeting apps can also help you monitor your spending and track your savings progress. They can send you alerts when you exceed your budget or when bills are due.

Try not to compare your own financial situation to someone else's. Each person's financial circumstances are different.

Dealing with Unexpected Expenses

One strategy for dealing with unexpected expenses is to create an emergency fund within your budget. Your emergency fund should cover at least three to six months of your regular expenses.

Finding other sources of income, such as taking on a weekend job or offering to help out a neighbor, can also help you offset unexpected expenses. If you can't pay back a bank or lender on time, it's sometimes possible to negotiate payment

29

plans. You can ask a parent, teacher, or other trusted adult for help with this.

Revising Your Budget

Unexpected expenses and events can disrupt your financial goals and require a change in your budget. Whatever the case, if your financial goals change, so must your budget.

Perhaps you got a raise at work or got another part-time job. When your income increases, revise your budget by allocating the additional funds wisely. If your income decreases, you may need to cut back on some expenses.

It is also a good idea to examine your current budget from time to time to determine what is and is not working. Are there expense categories where you're overspending or where you can cut back?

Advanced Budgeting Strategies

Cut Back on Unnecessary Expenses

One of the easiest ways to save money is to not spend it. But how do you know which expenses are necessary and which are not?

A need is a good or service that is essential to your survival or well-being, such as food and water, shelter, and health care. A want, or unnecessary expense, is a good or service you would like to have but is not essential to your survival or well-being, such as a new outfit or the latest smartphone. Before spending money on wants, make sure you have paid for your essentials first.

How to Make a Vision Board

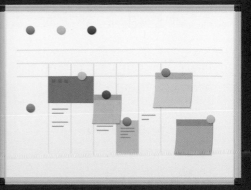

1
- Write down your goals
- Begin by jotting down your goals for these these five categories:

  -Spiritual   -Professional   -Recreational
  -Physical   -Relational

2
- Plan your strategies
- Provide a path to success by defining your actionable steps

3
- Add visuals
- Choose any visual that speaks to your future and serves as a reminder of your future dreams

4
- Arrange your goals, strategies, and visuals on the board

A Guide to Building an Emergency Fund

1. *Get a part-time job:* Find ways to earn money after school, on weekends, or during the summer.
2. *Save gift money:* Put a portion of gift money you receive for birthdays, holidays, and other occasions into your emergency fund.
3. *Do different household chores or jobs:* Perform different jobs for neighbors or family members, such as babysitting, mowing lawns, or pet sitting. Put the earned money into your emergency fund.
4. *Cut back on expenses:* Consider packing your lunch instead of buying food at school or work, or shop at thrift stores rather than buy new clothes. Put the money you save into your emergency fund.
5. *Participate in savings challenges:* Start a 52-week money challenge or a 365-day penny challenge. Sticking to the challenge can help you build your emergency fund over time.

Shop Around for the Best Deals

Shopping around for the best deals can help you cut your expenses. Researching different products and comparing prices while looking for sales, discounts, and coupons can save money on necessary items.

Cook More and Eat Out Less

Home-cooked meals are cheaper and healthier, and cooking can be a fun skill to practice! Explore recipes online or in cookbooks, and experiment with new flavors and ingredients. If your home has a coffee machine, consider making coffee instead of driving to a coffee shop.

Pause or Cancel Subscription Services

Subscriptions like streaming services and monthly gift boxes are fun and entertaining, but their costs can quickly accumulate. Examine your subscriptions closely and consider canceling the ones you rarely use.

Avoid Impulse Purchases

Impulse purchases are nonessential, unplanned purchases. Before purchasing things such as clothing, technology, or games, wait a week and ask yourself if you still want it. If the answer is yes, add the purchase to your budget and save up for it.

CHAPTER FOUR

How to Save Money

Saving money can be fun and rewarding, like completing quests in a video game. Completing quests often results in experience or points that can be used to purchase new gear, equipment, and other items. It can be exciting to watch these points go up, and it often helps players access new parts of the game. In real life, you can complete chores or work a job to earn money to spend on the things you want and need. This can also feel exciting and rewarding while helping you achieve your financial goals. In this chapter, you'll explore different strategies and techniques that can make saving money an exciting journey.

Short-Term Savings

Short-term savings are funds set aside for a specific purpose occurring in the near future. Some common examples include going on a vacation, taking a school trip, making a special one-time purchase, or buying holiday gifts for friends and family. To figure out what your short-term goals are, think about

Purchasing a birthday gift for a family member is a short-term goal. Making a list of gift ideas can help you decide how much you want to spend and how long you'll need to save.

the things you want to do or buy soon, and choose the most important ones to focus on.

Look at your income and expenses to determine the amount you can save monthly. Then create a plan to automatically transfer that amount into your savings account each month. Paying yourself first, or putting money into savings before you spend it on anything else, makes your savings goals the priority.

35

Long-Term Savings

Long-term savings are funds set aside for a significant expense or event occurring in the distant future. These savings are intended to assist you in meeting long-term financial goals and accumulating wealth over time. You might use long-term savings if you want to move out on your own, buy a car, or pay for college.

Strategies for Achieving Long-Term Savings Goals

Saving over a long period of time requires careful planning and discipline. One strategy to help you prioritize your financial future is to "pay yourself first." Paying yourself first means saving or investing a portion of your income before paying bills or other expenses. Investment is the act of putting your money into bonds, stocks, mutual funds, and other long-term savings accounts. Investment accounts grow your savings over time. We'll learn more about investing in Chapter 5.

Understanding Emergency Savings

Your emergency savings is the amount you set aside for emergencies or unexpected expenses. It is a safety net to avoid debt or financial crises when unexpected events occur. This money is not meant for daily expenses or entertainment. The idea of emergency savings is to "save when you don't need it, and it'll be there for you when you do," according to Frank Sonnenberg in *The Path to a Meaningful Life*.

For instance, if you lose your job, an emergency fund can help you pay bills and living expenses while you look for a new job. You can also use an emergency fund to pay medical expenses not covered by insurance if you get into an accident or have a medical emergency.

Tips for Saving Money

Building an emergency fund takes time and discipline. Here are some strategies to consider in building an emergency savings fund:

- *Determine how much you need to save:* Many financial experts recommend saving to cover three to six months of living expenses.
- *Set a savings goal:* After determining the amount to be saved, set a specific goal and a timeline. For instance, if you need $3,600 of emergency funds, you would need to save $300 a month for a year. Knowing your income and expenses can help you determine how much money to save and how long it will take to save it.
- *Store your savings in a separate account:* Most banks allow you to keep a savings account separate from your regular checking account. Putting your emergency funds in a savings account can help you avoid using it for other things.
- *Automate your savings:* Set up an automatic monthly transfer from your checking account to your emergency savings account. That way, you won't spend that money on anything else or forget a payment.

High-Yield Savings Accounts

When you put money into a savings account, the bank pays you interest for keeping your money there. Interest is basically free money that the bank gives you for leaving your money in their care. The interest rate, which the bank sets, determines how much interest you earn. If you have $100 in your savings account with a 5 percent yearly interest rate, you'll receive $5 in interest each year. While that may not seem like a lot, it adds up over time.

Savings accounts that offer higher interest rates than traditional savings accounts are called high-yield savings accounts. High-yield savings accounts provide higher interest rates, so you can earn more money from your savings. The interest you earn over time can rapidly increase and help you reach your savings goals.

Think Savings Goals: Additional Reasons for Saving

1. *Car Maintenance:* Purchasing a car is a big accomplishment, but maintenance and repair are other things to consider saving for.
2. *Paying for College:* Saving money for college ahead of time may keep you from taking on extra student loans.
3. *Supporting Family Expenses:* A contribution to a family emergency fund may ease financial burdens and ensure your family is financially secure.
4. *Living on Your Own:* Moving out can be an expensive undertaking. You'll have rent, utilities, and other bills to pay. A savings account or emergency fund will give you a leg up on these expenses.
5. *Fun Activities and Events:* Treat yourself by saving money to do the things you love, such as planning a camping trip or paying for an art class. This is your reward for being responsible with your finances.

Speaking with an account specialist at a bank or credit union is an effective way to decide which savings account is right for you.

Finding a high-yield savings account may require some research. To find the best high-yield savings account for you, it's important to do your research. Visit banks and credit unions, check their websites, or call them to compare their interest rates, requirements, and possible restrictions. You can also consider online banks, which might offer higher interest rates. Sometimes online banks also have fewer fees and lower minimum balance requirements.

Don't forget to read the fine print before you open an account. Make sure you understand the requirements and restrictions of the high-yield savings account before opening it. You may want to read through them with a parent, guardian, or other adult with financial experience who can point out important issues or considerations. Pay attention to any fees, minimum balance requirements, and withdrawal limitations.

CHAPTER FIVE
Investing Basics

nvesting is a tool that can multiply your hard-earned savings when used with care. Investing is not only for adults with a lot of money. Starting to invest as a teen or young adult can help you build wealth over time. In this chapter, we'll explore the basic concepts of investment.

Let's say you have a friend who is an artist. They tell you they need some money to buy supplies for their artwork. You agree to lend them money, and they promise to pay you back with interest after selling their art. Over time, your friend sells several of the paintings they made with those supplies. Your friend ends up paying you way more than you initially lent them! This is like how investing money can help you generate a big financial return over time.

Types of Investments

Some people pay money to invest in companies and other organizations. These organizations can use this money to hire more employees or grow in other ways. This is called investing.

221.90	•	-3.99				60
112.56	•	-2.57	-2.2%	114.81	111.93	228
3716.78	•	-148.50	-3.8%	3879.65	3696.4	571
282.04	•	-17.08	-5.7%	298.69	282.04	571
93.57	•	-3.19	-3.3%	96.75	93.57	207
89.93	•	-1.03	-1.1%	91.17	89.47	356
1019.23	•	-57.62	-5.4%	1077.38	1019.23	334
1457.56	•	-40.92	-2.7%	1503.79	1457.54	8,278
71.54	•	-1.43	-2.0%	72.96	71.44	891
3320.78	•	-105.40	-3.1%	3417.92	3320.78	891
133.27	•	-4.14	-3.0%	137.21	133.27	245
5648.86	•	-128.45	-2.2%	5774.98	5648.86	270
2517.48	•	-115.56	-4.4%	2600		1 26.5

A stock ticker is an electronic list of transactions and price changes for stocks. Tickers are updated continuously and provide investors with a clear picture of the stock market.

You can invest your money in many different forms, including stocks, bonds, mutual funds, and index funds.

When you buy stock in a company, you own a piece of that company. One piece is called one share. The value of your shares will go up and down based on how the company performs.

When you buy a bond, you loan an amount of money to a company or a government entity. In return, the borrower will give you back the money you invested, plus interest, at a specific future date.

Mutual funds are investments that allow you to combine your money with other people's money to buy many different types of things, such as stocks, bonds, and other assets. A professional manager takes care of choosing and managing these investments for you.

An index fund is a type of mutual fund that tracks one index, or one category, of the stock market. It is low-cost and can be lower-risk than investing in one single company. You can invest in an index fund by opening an account with a brokerage or investment platform and buying shares of the fund. It's a way to be part of the stock market without relying on just one company, and it's usually a cheaper option too.

Risk is the degree of uncertainty, potential of losing money, and failure to achieve the expected returns. Investing always involves risk. A good investor needs to weigh potential risks with potential rewards to make a smart decision.

Generating Returns

Investments generate returns, the profit or loss earned from an investment over time. This is a form of passive income. Passive income is money you earn passively, or without directly working for it. Bonds, dividend income from stocks, and rental income from real estate investments are examples of passive income. Investing in these assets can be one way to make money.

When some companies make a big profit, they pay their investors back in dividends. If you own a stock in a company, you might receive a dividend at the end of the year or quarter. Dividends can be a reliable source of income for long-term investors. While not all companies pay dividends, many large and established companies do. But dividend payments are not guaranteed. They can change depending on if the company has a good or bad financial year.

When it comes to investing, compound interest plays an

important role in helping your money grow over time. While some companies reward their investors with dividends, which are a share of their profits, not all companies provide this income. However, even if you don't receive dividends, you can still benefit from compound interest.

Compound interest is a concept that applies to various types of investments. It means that the interest you earn on your initial investment can, in turn, earn additional interest over time. For example, an investment account with $1,000 and a 5 percent annual interest would earn $50 interest during the first year. The next year, that $1,050 will earn $52.50. Over time, you can earn more and more. This compounding effect can significantly increase the value of your investment.

The Five Basic Principles of Investing

Investing can be a complex and risky process. But you can maximize your success and minimize your risk by understanding these five basic investment principles.

- *Diversification:* Diversification means not putting all your eggs in one basket. Instead of investing all your money in one thing, like one company or one type of investment, you spread your money across different types of investments. This helps reduce the risk of losing all your money if one company or investment strategy doesn't do well.
- *Time horizon:* A time horizon is how long you plan to hold onto your investment before cashing out. If you're investing for a long time, perhaps

10 or 20 years, you can take more risks because you have more time to recover from any losses. But if you need the money in a year or two, you might want to choose safer investments.

- *Risk tolerance:* Risk tolerance is how much risk you're comfortable with. Some people enjoy taking risks and might be okay with investing in stocks that can go up and down a lot. Other people might prefer safer investments, such as bonds. It's important to choose investments that match your risk tolerance.

- *Buy low, sell high:* This means buying an investment when the price is low, and then selling it when the price is higher. It's a good strategy for making money, but it can be hard to predict when prices will go up or down.

- *Always take profit:* When you make money on an investment, it's important to take some of that money out and put it in your pocket. That way, even if the investment goes down later, you still made some money. As Idowu Koyenikan writes in *Wealth for All: Living a Life of Success at the Edge of Your Ability*, "the more your money works for you, the less you have to work for money."

Choosing the Right Investment Account

An investment account is a type of account where you can hold cash and purchase investments such as stocks, bonds, and mutual funds. There are different types of investment accounts:

- *Individual retirement accounts (IRAs):* IRAs are special accounts that help you save money for your retirement. With a traditional IRA, you can deduct the money you put in from your taxes now, but you'll pay taxes on it when you take it out in retirement. With a Roth IRA, you don't get a tax break for putting the money in now, but you won't have to pay any taxes on the money you take out in retirement.

- *401(k) plans:* A 401(k) plan is a retirement savings plan sponsored by employers. This allows employees to save a part of their paycheck before taxes for retirement.

- *High-yield savings accounts:* These savings accounts offer a higher interest rate than traditional savings accounts.

- *Treasury bonds:* Treasury bonds are a safe way to invest your money. They are offered by the government. When you buy a treasury bond, you're lending money to the government. The government will pay you back with interest at a fixed time in the future.

- *Certificates of deposit (CDs):* CDs are considered low-risk savings accounts that offer a fixed rate of return over a period of time ranging from a few months to several years.

- *Taxable investment accounts:* These are regular accounts that allow you to buy and sell stocks, bonds, and other investments. Unlike retirement accounts, they do not have any special tax advantages. But they offer more freedom in

terms of when you can take out money and how
you choose to invest it.

Table 2. Tax Benefits and Rules of Investment Accounts		
Type of Account	Tax Benefits	Rules
Individual retirement accounts (IRAs)	Tax breaks for contributions and growth. Roth IRAs allow tax-free withdrawals in retirement.	Limits on contributions and withdrawals. Early withdrawals before age 59½ may be subject to penalties and taxes.
401(k) plans	Tax breaks for contributions and growth.	Limits on contributions and withdrawals. Early withdrawals before age 59½ may be subject to penalties and taxes.
High-yield savings accounts	Higher interest rates than regular savings accounts.	Limits on withdrawals. FDIC-insured*.
Treasury bonds	Interest earned is not taxed by state and local governments.	Minimum investment of $100. Interest is paid every six months until maturity.
CDs	Higher interest rates than regular savings accounts.	Fixed term with penalties for early withdrawal. FDIC-insured.
Taxable investment accounts	No tax breaks.	No limits on contributions or withdrawals. Gains and losses are taxed when investments are sold.

* FDIC-insured means that a bank account is backed by the Federal Deposit Insurance Corporation (FDIC) up to a certain amount of money. This means that if the bank fails, the account holder will not lose their deposited funds up to the FDIC-insured limit.

Tips for Making Budgeting Work for You

Inflation happens when prices go up. Even though things get more expensive, you might not make more income. Inflation makes it harder to purchase things you need and requires you to adjust your budget accordingly. For example, if you usually budget $10 for a bus pass, and the price goes up to $12.50, you'll need to move $2.50 from a different part of your budget.

Inflation and investing are closely related. Inflation reduces the purchasing power of money, affects interest rates, and influences how much investments are worth.

You can't avoid inflation, but there are strategies you can use to understand how inflation affects you. It's important to have diverse investments. A combination might include stocks, real estate, and commodities. Commodities are physical assets such as gold, oil, and crops that can keep their value when prices increase.

CHAPTER SIX
Exploring Cryptocurrency

C ryptocurrency has gained a lot of attention in recent years. Cryptocurrency is a type of digital money that's different from traditional currency, such as US dollars ($) or Japanese yen (¥). One way that it's different is that you can't touch or see cryptocurrency. It is similar to a video game currency. Another difference is that cryptocurrency is *decentralized*. This means it isn't controlled or backed by a person or government the way most currencies are.

Cryptocurrency can be used anytime and anywhere in the world without the need for banks or credit card companies. Some people made a lot of money investing in cryptocurrencies that became very valuable over time. However, cryptocurrency can also be very risky. While some people have made huge profits from cryptocurrency, many people have lost money investing in digital currencies. Some people have even lost millions of dollars by investing in cryptocurrency. In this chapter, we'll explore the basics of cryptocurrency, including the risks, rewards, and different currencies on the market.

Bitcoin was created in 2009. The currency is stored in a digital wallet that is protected by a secure password.

The Basics of Cryptocurrency

Cryptocurrencies have seen explosive growth since Bitcoin appeared in 2009. There are an estimated 23,000 different types of cryptocurrencies in existence around the world. Unlike traditional currency, cryptocurrency is not physical money. Instead, it exists in a digital form. Cryptocurrency can be bought, sold, and traded much like stocks and other investments.

Cryptocurrencies such as Bitcoin are created through a process called mining, where powerful computers solve complex math problems. Miners compete to solve these problems and are rewarded with new Bitcoins. Cryptocurrencies are valuable because they offer decentralized transactions, limited supply, and secure transactions.

Certain cryptocurrencies are used for specific purposes, including purchasing video games and art or gaining access to virtual worlds sometimes called the metaverse. The metaverse is a digital universe that is created and run by users where people can interact, play games, and do other activities without being physically near each other. Other

In the metaverse, users can socialize, play games, and make purchases virtually. The metaverse allows people to have experiences they may not be able to access in the physical world.

cryptocurrencies, such as Bitcoin, can be used to buy just about anything. People have used Bitcoin to purchase groceries, plane tickets, music, and more. The acceptance of cryptocurrencies for everyday purchases may vary, but their potential to be used as a form of payment continues to expand.

The Benefits and Risks of Cryptocurrency

Cryptocurrency offers a low entry price compared to larger investments like buying a house. With cryptocurrency, an investor can buy any amount of a single coin—even just a tiny part of one coin. This means you can invest in cryptocurrency even with a minimal amount of money.

However, investing in cryptocurrency is extremely risky compared to most traditional stocks or investments. The value of cryptocurrency can change dramatically. It's possible to lose all your investments overnight.

Cryptocurrency is still largely unregulated. It operates independently from traditional financial systems and governments, making it difficult to establish consistent rules. Thus, it poses a higher risk of fraud than other investments. People can lose a lot of money in cryptocurrency. Fake cryptocurrencies, scams, and inflated prices have left some investors with nothing.

Finally, one of the most significant disadvantages of cryptocurrency is the environmental impact of digital mining. Mining cryptocurrency requires a lot of computing power, which demands a lot of energy. This energy consumption means electric companies must burn more coal or natural gas to meet the needs of these servers. Many people concerned about the environment are against mining cryptocurrency because it releases huge amounts of greenhouse gases into the atmosphere, contributing to or potentially even worsening global warming.

Types of Cryptocurrencies

Cryptocurrencies can be categorized into four main types, each with unique features, uses, and risks. The first type of cryptocurrency is blue-chip coins. These coins have a history dating back to the early 2010s and are the most established

Bitcoin mining requires massive computer systems. Miners use these computers to solve complex math problems, which results in new coins.

cryptocurrencies. Bitcoin (BTC) and Ethereum (ETH) are the most popular blue-chip coins. These coins are considered the safest and most reliable because of their stability and history.

Stablecoins are the second type of cryptocurrency. These coins are linked to a stable asset, such as the US dollar. This is done in an attempt to keep the coins' value stable, reducing how much the price goes up or down. However, it's important to note that stability is not always guaranteed, and these investments are not FDIC-insured.

Altcoins are cryptocurrencies that are alternatives to Bitcoin and Ethereum. They are often used for specific purposes and are still being tested in the marketplace. Ripple (XRP) and Sandbox (SAND) are examples of altcoins. Since altcoins have yet to prove themselves in the market, they are riskier than traditional investments.

Finally, meme coins are cryptocurrencies based on internet memes. They usually have no real purpose or value. Dogecoin (DOGE) and Shiba Inu (SHIB) coins are examples of meme coins. These are very risky, and buying them is similar to gambling at a casino. These are not recommended for new investors because an investor could easily and quickly lose everything they invest.

CONCLUSION
The Bottom Line

Throughout this book, you've learned about budgeting, saving, investing, and even cryptocurrency. By taking the time to develop these skills and knowledge, you can take control of your finances and work toward achieving your financial goals.

Budgeting is the first step toward financial stability. Budgeting helps you make wise financial decisions and improve your financial outlook for the long term. Building good budgeting habits early on can help you avoid common money mistakes and reach your goals faster.

Saving money is another essential skill. By saving regularly and taking advantage of opportunities to grow your money, you can create a financial cushion and be ready for unexpected costs.

Investing can boost your budget and help you reach your financial goals. You learned about different types of investments, such as stocks, bonds, and mutual funds, and how to analyze them to make wise investment decisions.

Knowing the basics about money management and financial planning can prepare you for big purchases down the road.

Cryptocurrency is an alternative investment opportunity with potential risks and benefits. You learned about the basics of cryptocurrency, including how it's different from other types of money.

Having your own money helps you learn independence and self-reliance. Knowing you can set and reach a financial goal is a great feeling!

College Fund

You can always go back and reread any chapter in this book to remember what you learned. But here are a few final points to keep in mind:

- Set realistic financial goals and create a budget that fits your unique financial situation.
- Build good budgeting habits early on to avoid common financial pitfalls.
- Save consistently and take advantage of opportunities to grow your money.
- Assess investment options, such as stocks, bonds, and mutual funds, to make good investment decisions.
- Understand the risks and benefits of cryptocurrency and manage these risks to make informed investment decisions.

Beginning the process of budgeting may be challenging for you. But as Manoj Arora writes in *From the Rat Race to Financial Freedom*, "coming out of your comfort zone is tough in the beginning, chaotic in the middle, awesome in the end . . . because in the end, it shows you a whole new world." Remember, it takes time and discipline to build good financial habits, but the efforts are well worth it. By staying committed and knowledgeable, you can achieve financial freedom and stability.

GLOSSARY

bonds: a way for individuals or investors to save money by lending it to someone else, such as a company or the government

commodity: an economic good, product, or raw material

compound interest: interest that is earned on both the principal amount of money saved and the interest that money has already earned

cryptocurrency: a digital currency with no central regulating authority that uses encryption for security and a decentralized system to record transactions

debt: money that is owed to another person, organization, or government

diversification: the act of spreading out money across different types of investments or assets

dividend: a portion of a company's profits that is paid out to its shareholders as a form of return on their investment

financial freedom: the ability to live the life a person wants without worrying about money

financial literacy: the knowledge and skills needed to manage money effectively

401(k) plan: a type of retirement savings plan offered by employers to which employees and employers can contribute on which taxes are deferred until withdrawal

income: money that comes in from a job, business, or property

index fund: a type of investment fund that allows individuals or investors to pool their money together to invest in a diverse collection of stocks that track a specific stock market index, such as the S&P 500

individual retirement account (IRA): a type of savings account designed to help people save for retirement

interest: a charge for borrowed money paid by the borrower or to an investor

investment: putting money into something with the expectation of making a profit

investment account: a type of account that allows a person to invest in various assets

lender: a person, organization, or financial institution that lends money to another person, often with the expectation of receiving repayment plus interest

mortgage: a loan used to buy a house or property that is paid back over time with interest

mutual fund: an investment company that pools money from many individuals to purchase a variety of stocks, bonds, or other assets

passive income: money earned through investments or other sources that require little or no effort to maintain

profit: money earned after all expenses have been paid

real estate: property consisting of land or buildings that can be bought, sold, or rented for use

returns: the profit or loss earned from an investment over a period of time

risk tolerance: a person's willingness or ability to take financial risks

savings account: a bank account where a person can deposit money and earn interest over time

spreadsheet: a computer program used to store, organize, and analyze financial data

stock: a type of investment that represents partial ownership in a company

supply: the amount of particular good or service that is available for purchase at any given time

SOURCE NOTES

6   "telling your money where to go.": Oxenreider, Tsh. *Organized Simplicity: The Clutter-Free Approach to Intentional Living*. Betterway Home, 2010.

17   "When money realizes . . . in those hands.": Koyenika, Idowu. *Wealth for All: Living a Life of Success at the Edge of Your Ability*. Fuquay Varina, NC: Grandeur Touch, LLC, 2016.

19   "spending money to . . . have less money.": Housel, Morgan. *The Psychology of Money*. Hampshire, Great Britain: Harriman House, 2020.

4   "save when you . . . when you do.": Sonnenberg, Frank. *The Path to a Meaningful Life*, 2022.

5   "the more your . . . work for money.": Koyenikan, Idowu. *Wealth for All: Living a Life of Success at the Edge of Your Ability*. Fuquay Varina, NC: Grandeur Touch, LLC, 2016.

57   "coming out of . . . whole new world.": Arora, Manoj. *From the Rat Race to Financial Freedom*. Mumbai: Jaico Publishing House, 2013.

SELECTED BIBLIOGRAPHY

Bodie, Zvi, Alex Kane, and Alan Marcus. *Investments*. New York: McGraw Hill, 2017.

Cruze, Rachel. *Know Yourself, Know Your Money*. Franklin, TN: Ramsey Press, 2021.

Malkiel, Burton G. *A Random Walk down Wall Street: The Time-tested Strategy for Successful Investing*. New York: W. W. Norton & Company, 2016.

Mishkin, Frederic. *Economics of Money, Banking and Financial Markets, The Business School Edition*. Toronto: Pearson, 2018.

Rapley, Tonya B. *The Money Manual: A Practical Money Guide to Help You Succeed On Your Financial Journey*. North Charleston, SC: CreateSpace Independent Publishing Platform, 2018.

Sabatier, Grant. *Financial Freedom: A Proven Path to All the Money You Will Ever Need*. Avery, 2020.

FURTHER READING

Books

Chatzky, Jean, and Kathryn Tuggle. *How to Money: Your Ultimate Visual Guide to the Basics of Finance*. New York: Roaring Brook Press, 2022.
A comprehensive finance guide that provides readers with a visual approach to understanding the basics of personal finance. This book covers a wide range of topics, including budgeting, saving, investing, and managing debt. With its visual aids and easy-to-understand language, it is an excellent resource for individuals looking to enhance their financial literacy and make informed decisions about money.

Hayes, Kevin. *Financial Literacy Information for Teens*. Detroit: Omnigraphics, Inc., 2021.
This book aims to educate young readers about essential financial concepts and equip them with the knowledge and skills necessary to make sound financial decisions as they transition into adulthood. Covering topics such as budgeting, banking, credit, and saving, this book serves as a valuable resource for teenagers who want to develop a strong foundation in financial literacy.

Housel, Morgan. *The Psychology of Money: Timeless Lessons on Wealth, Greed, and Happiness*. Hampshire: Harriman House. 2021.
An insightful and thought-provoking exploration of the complex relationship between human psychology and finance. Drawing on his experience as a financial journalist and investor, Housel delves into the behavioral aspects that influence our financial decisions, demonstrating how emotions, biases, and perceptions shape the way we handle money.

Hung, Michelle. *Investing for Teens: How to Save, Invest, and Grow Money*. Oakland: Rockridge Press, 2022.
Focuses on the importance of saving, investing, and growing money. This book provides practical guidance on how to develop good financial habits, understand investment strategies, and make informed decisions to secure their financial future. With its clear explanations and actionable advice, it empowers young readers to take control of their finances and start building wealth at an early age.

Sethi, Ramit. *I Will Teach You to Be Rich: No Guilt. No Excuses. Just a 6-Week Program That Works*. New York: Workman Publishing Company. 2019.
A practical and engaging personal finance guide. Sethi presents a six-week program that aims to help readers take control of their finances and achieve financial success without guilt or excuses.

Websites

Biz Kids

https://bizkids.com/

An Emmy Award-winning television series and website that teaches about money and business. The website offers videos, games, and activities to help teens understand concepts like entrepreneurship, investing, saving, and making smart financial choices. It provides practical information in a fun and engaging format.

Money as You Grow

https://www.consumerfinance.gov/consumer-tools/money-as-you-grow/

A website created by the Consumer Financial Protection Bureau (CFPB) to help parents and educators teach children about money. The site offers age-appropriate lessons and activities to help kids develop important financial skills, including budgeting and saving.

Practical Money Skills for Life

https://www.practicalmoneyskills.com/

Provides comprehensive financial education resources for teens. The website offers interactive tools, articles, and calculators to help teens learn about budgeting, saving, investing, and making smart financial decisions.

Smart About Money

https://www.smartaboutmoney.org/Courses/Money-Basics-for-Teens

A website that offers courses and resources on personal finance. Their course on Money Basics for Teens covers topics such as budgeting, saving, and managing credit, and is designed to be engaging and interactive for young people.

Teens' Guide to Building a Strong Personal Finance Foundation

https://www.moneygeek.com/financial-planning/personal-finance-for-teens/

Offers advice and information on a range of financial topics. Their guide for teens and money includes tips and advice on budgeting, saving, and investing.

INDEX

ABOUT THE AUTHOR

Dr. Nicholas Suivski is a finance, business, and phonics writer with an entrepreneurial spirit. He has owned multiple businesses and is a practicing doctor of physical therapy. Now, he focuses on writing and business development roles. Past books he has written include *Defining Money in the Age of Cryptocurrency, Investing with Cryptocurrency: How to Buy, Sell, and Save, The Future of Cryptocurrency*, and *Scholarly Jim*. When Nicholas is not writing and working, he enjoys snowboarding, hiking, soccer, and driving cars.

PHOTO ACKNOWLEDGMENTS

FatCamera/Getty Images, p.5; Dragon Images/Shutterstock, p.7; JGI/ Jamie Grill/Getty Images, p.10; Peter Dazeley/Getty Images, p.15; Ekaterina Podrezova/Getty Images, p.17; Alvaro Medina Jurado/Getty Images, p.18; Casper1774 Studio/Shutterstock, p.20; Charles Gullung/ Getty Images, p.25; Odua Images/Shutterstock, p.35; BulentBARIS/ Getty Images, p.39; EDUARD MUZHEVSKYI/SCIENCE PHOTO LIBRARY/ Getty Images, p.41; Andriy Onufriyenko/Getty Images, p.47; Koron/ Getty Images, p.49; Yagi Studio/Getty Images, p.50; Mark Agnor/ Shutterstock, p.52; Krakenimages.com/Shutterstock, p.55; Design Pics/ Design Pics CEF/Getty Images, p.56

Cover image: fizkes/Shutterstock